Baby animals on islands

Bobbie Kalman
Crabtree Publishing Company
www.crabtreebooks.com

The Habitats of Baby Animals

Created by Bobbie Kalman

For Maelle Eve Pohorly
You are the sunshine that lights up
your family's life.

Author and Editor-in-Chief
Bobbie Kalman

Editor
Kathy Middleton

Proofreader
Crystal Sikkens

Design
Bobbie Kalman
Katherine Berti
Samantha Crabtree
(front cover)

Photo research
Bobbie Kalman

Print and production coordinator
Katherine Berti

Photographs
Bigstockphoto: title page
Expresiv Maps: p. 8–9 (map), 24 (continents)
ZSSD/Minden Pictures: p. 13 (right)
Wikimedia Commons: National Park Service,
    U.S. Department of the Interior: p. 10 (island fox kit),
    p. 23 (top left); PanBK: p. 21 (bottom right),
    24 (habitats)
All other images by Shutterstock

Library and Archives Canada Cataloguing in Publication

Kalman, Bobbie
    Baby animals on islands / Bobbie Kalman.

(The habitats of baby animals)
Includes index.
Issued also in electronic formats.
ISBN 978-0-7787-1016-5 (bound).--ISBN 978-0-7787-1027-1 (pbk.)

    1. Island animals--Infancy--Juvenile literature. 2. Island
ecology--Juvenile literature. I. Title. II. Series: Kalman, Bobbie.
Habitats of baby animals.

QL111.K34 2013   j591.3'9209142   C2012-908305-4

Library of Congress Cataloging-in-Publication Data

CIP available at Library of Congress

Crabtree Publishing Company

www.crabtreebooks.com   1-800-387-7650

Printed in Canada/012013/MA20121217

Published in Canada
Crabtree Publishing
616 Welland Ave.
St. Catharines, Ontario
L2M 5V6

Published in the United States
Crabtree Publishing
PMB 59051
350 Fifth Avenue, 59th Floor
New York, New York 10118

Published in the United Kingdom
Crabtree Publishing
Maritime House
Basin Road North, Hove
BN41 1WR

Published in Australia
Crabtree Publishing
3 Charles Street
Coburg North
VIC, 3058

What is in this book?

What is an island?

An **island** is an area of land that has water all around it. Islands are found all over the world in **oceans**, rivers, and lakes. Oceans are huge bodies of water that contain **salt water**. Rivers and lakes have **fresh water**. Some islands are huge. Some are tiny. Many kinds of animals live on islands. Some animals are found only on one island. Some are found in other places, too.

Some animals live in oceans around islands. Many kinds of fish, whales, sea turtles, and seals live in oceans. This manta ray and sea turtle find the food they need in the salt water of oceans.

sea turtle

manta ray

What is a habitat?

Different kinds of **habitats** can be found on islands in different parts of the world. **Forests** such as **rain forests** grow on many islands. **Deserts**, **grasslands**, and **tundras** are other habitats that are part of some islands.

Living and non-living

Habitats contain **living things** and **non-living things**. To stay alive, living things need both non-living things and other living things.

Many new words

The words on the right explain the meanings of some of the habitat words that appear in **bold** letters on these pages. They may be new to you.

Habitat words

desert A dry area that gets little rain or snow

forest An area with many trees and other plants

fresh water Water that contains very little salt

grassland A large area covered mainly in grasses

habitat A natural place where plants grow and animals live

living things Plants, animals, and people

non-living things Air, sunlight, water, soil, rocks

rain forest A forest that gets a lot of rain every day or during rainy seasons

salt water Water that contains a lot of salt

tundra A large treeless Arctic area with soil that is always frozen

What do they need?

Baby animals that live in island habitats learn to find the things they need to **survive**, or stay alive. They need food, water, and **shelter**. Shelter protects animals from bad weather and keeps them safe from **predators**. Predators are animals that hunt and eat other animals, especially baby animals.

*This baby arctic fox lives in a **den**, or home, under some rocks. The weather is cold where he lives. The den keeps him warm and safe from predators.*

Water to drink

All animals need to drink water. The oceans around islands contain salt water, but most islands also have fresh water that animals on land can drink.

What do they eat?

Some island animals are **herbivores**. Herbivores eat mainly plants. **Carnivores** eat other animals. Many carnivores are also predators. The animals they hunt are called **prey**. Animals that eat both plants and other animals are called **omnivores**. Arctic foxes are predators, but they also eat plants. Gibbons eat mainly plants, but they also eat other animals. Both are omnivores.

This mother macaque monkey and her baby have found fresh water to drink in their island habitat.

These gibbons eat mainly leaves and fruit, but they also eat insects, birds, and bird eggs.

7

Where on Earth?

Millions of **species**, or types, of animals live on islands. Islands can be found on every **continent**. A continent is a huge area of land on Earth. Earth's seven continents, from largest to smallest, are Asia, Africa, North America, South America, Antarctica, Europe, and Australia/Oceania. All these continents have islands.

Use this map!

This map will help you find the islands on which the animals in this book live.

Ellesmere Island
Greenland
Canada
Hecla Island
Baffin Island
San Juan Islands
North America
United States
Channel Islands
Atlantic Ocean
Galapagos Islands
South America
Pacific Ocean

Earth's five oceans, from largest to smallest, are the Pacific, Atlantic, Indian, Southern, and Arctic oceans. Find them on this map.

Hot and cold places

Some islands are near the **equator**. The equator is an imaginary line that divides Earth into two parts. The weather at the equator is always hot. There are also islands near the North Pole and South Pole. The weather in these places is cold for most of the year.

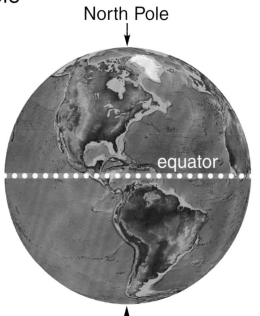

The North Pole is at the top of Earth. The South Pole is at the bottom of Earth. The equator is at the center of Earth.

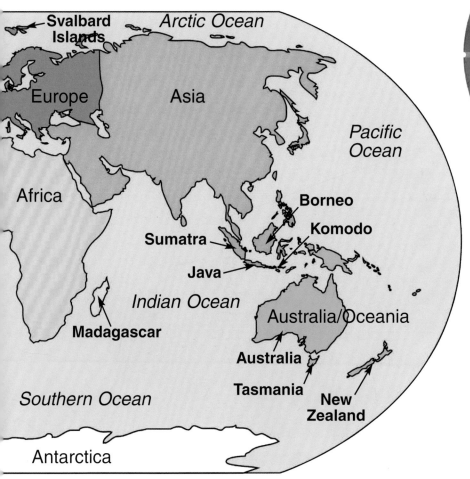

Island babies

Some of these baby animals live only
on certain islands. Others live both
on islands and on **mainland** areas,
or large land areas that are not islands.

baby
ringtail
lemur

Sumatran tiger cub

young crowned sifaka

island fox kit

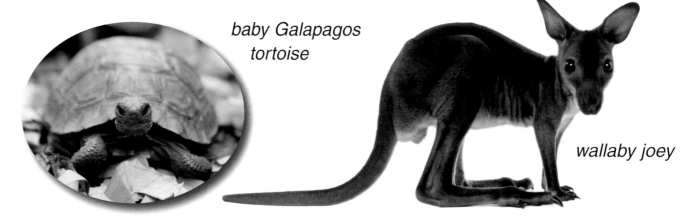

baby Galapagos
tortoise

wallaby joey

baby Sumatran orangutan

Galapagos sea lion pup

baby gibbon

arctic fox kit

polar bear cub

young brown kiwi

Only on Madagascar!

Madagascar is an island that is part of the continent of Africa. It is the only place where lemurs and some other animals can be found. Animals that live only in certain places are said to be **endemic** to those areas. The animals on these pages are endemic to Madagascar.

Mouse lemurs are as small as mice. They eat insects, fruit, flowers, and leaves.

*Many kinds of lemurs live on Madagascar. Some live in trees, and some, like these ring-tailed lemurs, live in big groups on the ground. The baby lemurs in this **troop**, or group, are protected by the adults all around them.*

This leaf-tailed gecko's tail and coloring provide **camouflage**. Camouflage helps animals blend in with their surroundings. Camouflage hides this gecko from the prey it hunts.

This young crowned sifaka is a kind of lemur. It can be found in the dry forests of Madagascar. The sifaka is known as the "dancing lemur" because it looks like it is dancing when it hops along the ground.

This baby fossa looks like a cat, but it is part of the mongoose family. Adult fossas are the largest predators on Madagascar. They hunt mainly lemurs, but they also eat lizards, birds, and small animals that live on farms.

Endangered animals

Indonesia is a country made up of about 17,508 islands, which are located at the equator. Hundreds of endemic animals live in Indonesia, and many are **endangered** because their forest habitats are being cut down. Endangered animals are in danger of disappearing from Earth forever. The baby animals on these pages live on the Indonesian islands of Sumatra, Java, and Borneo. Komodo dragons live only on five islands, including Komodo Island.

This tiger cub is one of about 500 Sumatran tigers left in the world. Much of the rain forest where the tigers once lived has been cut down.

Komodo dragons are huge lizards. They hunt their food, but they also eat animals other predators leave behind.

Orangutans, like this mother and baby, live in the rain forests of Sumatra and Borneo. They spend most of their time in trees.

Javan rhinoceros are among the most endangered animals on Earth, with fewer than 35 left. They live on the island of Java. People have hunted them for their horns.

Galapagos Islands

The Galapagos Islands are located at the equator in the Pacific Ocean. They are part of the country of Ecuador, in South America. Endemic Galapagos animals include the giant tortoise, marine iguanas, and Galapagos sea lions. These animals have all **adapted**, or changed, to survive on the islands on which they live. The sea lions are endangered, and the tortoises and iguanas are **vulnerable**, or at risk of becoming endangered.

This Galapagos sea lion pup was born over a week ago. Its mother stayed with it for the first week of its life, but she has now gone into the ocean to look for food. The pup waits for her on the beach. In another week, the pup will go into the ocean with her and start learning how to swim.

saddleback
shell

dome-shaped
shell

Galapagos giant tortoises live on seven of the islands. The shapes of their shells and necks are different from island to island. The tortoise on the left has a long neck and a saddleback shell. The other one has a dome-shaped shell and shorter neck.

The Galapagos marine iguana is the only type of iguana that eats plants mostly from the ocean. A baby iguana hangs on to this adult's back for protection.

17

Islands in the north

If you look at the map on pages 8–9, you will see many large islands in the northern part of Earth, called the Arctic. Some of these islands are Greenland, Baffin Island and Ellesmere Island in Canada, and Svalbard, a group of islands north of Norway. Baby animals such as polar bear cubs, arctic fox kits, and many kinds of birds can be found on all these islands. These animals also live in mainland Arctic habitats.

Arctic terns fly from the Arctic to the South Pole and back each year. This **chick**, or baby bird, will fly south with its mother at the end of the summer.

arctic fox kit

Arctic foxes, like the fox kit on the left, live on Arctic islands and mainlands. In winter, this kit will have thick white fur to keep it warm, like the adult fox on the right.

adult arctic fox

The Arctic tundra habitat is a cold desert where no trees grow.

These polar bear cubs and their mother have two layers of thick fur, as well as a layer of fat called **blubber**.

19

Way down south

Australia and New Zealand are in the southern part of Earth. Australia has several islands. Tasmania is one of them. New Zealand has two main islands, North Island and South Island, and several smaller islands.

Babies called joeys

Many animals on these islands are **marsupials**. Most marsupial mothers have a **pouch**, or pocket, where their babies grow. The joeys, or babies, live in the pouches and drink their mothers' milk. They leave the pouches when they are ready to find food and live on their own.

Brushtail possums live in forests on Australian and New Zealand islands. These small marsupials are omnivores that eat plants, insects, and eggs.

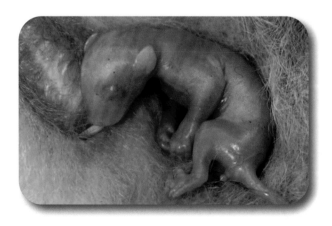

This tiny brushtail possum joey is drinking milk inside its mother's pouch.

Wallabies are smaller than kangaroos. They live in grasslands with bushes that are near forests. This wallaby joey has left its mother's pouch to look for food.

Kiwis are birds that cannot fly. They are endemic to New Zealand. This young kiwi is a North Island brown kiwi.

This Tasmanian devil lives on the island of Tasmania, which is part of Australia. It is a fierce predator. It also eats prey caught by other predators.

Forest wallabies are called pademelons. They are the smallest wallabies. This mother and joey live on Tasmania.

Foxes on islands

Foxes live in many kinds of habitats all over the world, such as the Arctic tundra, but some foxes, like the island foxes on the opposite page, live only on certain islands. The fox kits on these pages live on islands in the United States and Canada. Some of the islands are in the Pacific Ocean. One is located in a lake.

The San Juan Islands are between the state of Washington in the United States, and Vancouver Island, in Canada. Long ago, settlers from Europe brought rabbits to these islands for food. Soon, there were too many rabbits, so they brought foxes to hunt them. This lovely red fox kit lives on one of the San Juan islands, along with many rabbits, like the ones below.

island fox kit

adult
island fox

Island foxes are small gray foxes that live only on six Channel Islands, off the coast of California. They are **critically endangered**, or close to dying out.

This red fox mother and her kit live on Hecla Island. Hecla Island is in Lake Winnipeg, in Manitoba, Canada.

Words to know and Index

babies

continents
pages 8–9,
12

**endangered
animals**
pages 14–15,
16, 23

Arctic
pages 5, 6, 7, 8,
9, 11, 18–19, 22

pages 6, 7, 10–11,
12, 13, 14, 15, 16, 17,
18, 19, 20, 21, 22, 23

foxes
pages 6, 10, 11,
18, 19, 22–23

habitats
pages 5, 6, 7,
14, 18, 19, 22

marsupials
page 20

mothers
pages 7, 15, 16,
18, 19, 20, 21, 23

oceans
pages 4, 7, 8, 9,
16, 17, 22